COUNT IT ALL JOY!

COUNT IT ALL JOY!

DEDICATED TO MY PHENOMENAL SON, CHRISTIAN MCGHEE.

THIS JOURNAL BELONGS TO

....

DATE: S M T W TH F S ___ ___ ___

I AM THANKFUL FOR

1 

2 

3 ____________________

TODAY I FEEL

WRITE OR DRAW ABOUT
YOUR FAVORITE PART OF TODAY!

DATE: S M T W TH F S ____ ____ ____

I AM THANKFUL FOR

1. ______________________________

2. ______________________________

3. ______________________________

TODAY I FEEL

WRITE OR DRAW ABOUT YOUR FAVORITE PART OF TODAY!

DATE: S M T W TH F S ___ ___ ___

I AM THANKFUL FOR

1 ______________________

2 ______________________

3 ______________________

TODAY I FEEL

WRITE OR DRAW ABOUT YOUR FAVORITE PART OF TODAY!

DATE: S M T W TH F S ___ ___ ___

I AM THANKFUL FOR

1 ______

2 ______

3 ______

TODAY I FEEL

WRITE OR DRAW ABOUT
YOUR FAVORITE PART OF TODAY!

DATE: S M T W TH F S ___ ___ ___

I AM THANKFUL FOR

1 ______________________

2 ______________________

3 ______________________

TODAY I FEEL

WRITE OR DRAW ABOUT
YOUR FAVORITE PART OF TODAY!

A JOYFUL MOMENT

TAKE A NATURE WALK WITH YOUR FAMILY. WHAT ARE SOME OF THE THINGS IN NATURE YOU ARE THANKFUL FOR?

DATE: S M T W TH F S ___ ___ ___

I AM THANKFUL FOR

1. ______________________________

2. ______________________________

3. ______________________________

TODAY I FEEL

WRITE OR DRAW ABOUT
YOUR FAVORITE PART OF TODAY!

DATE: S M T W TH F S ___ ___ ___

I AM THANKFUL FOR

1 ______

2 ______

3 ______

TODAY I FEEL

WRITE OR DRAW ABOUT
YOUR FAVORITE PART OF TODAY!

DATE: S M T W TH F S ___ ___ ___

I AM THANKFUL FOR

1 ______________________________

2 ______________________________

3 ______________________________

TODAY I FEEL

WRITE OR DRAW ABOUT
YOUR FAVORITE PART OF TODAY!

DATE: S M T W TH F S ___ ___ ___

I AM THANKFUL FOR

1 ______

2 ______

3 ______

TODAY I FEEL

WRITE OR DRAW ABOUT
YOUR FAVORITE PART OF TODAY!

DATE: S M T W TH F S ___ ___ ___

I AM THANKFUL FOR

1 ______________________

2 ______________________

3 ______________________

TODAY I FEEL

WRITE OR DRAW ABOUT
YOUR FAVORITE PART OF TODAY!

DATE: S M T W TH F S ___ ___ ___

I AM THANKFUL FOR

1. ______________________________

2. ______________________________

3. ______________________________

TODAY I FEEL

WRITE OR DRAW ABOUT
YOUR FAVORITE PART OF TODAY!

DATE: S M T W TH F S ____ ____ ____

I AM THANKFUL FOR

1 ____

2 ____

3 ____

TODAY I FEEL

WRITE OR DRAW ABOUT YOUR FAVORITE PART OF TODAY!

DATE: S M T W TH F S ____ ____ ____

I AM THANKFUL FOR

1 ____________________

2 ____________________

3 ____________________

TODAY I FEEL

WRITE OR DRAW ABOUT
YOUR FAVORITE PART OF TODAY!

DATE: S M T W TH F S ___ ___ ___

I AM THANKFUL FOR

1. ______________________________
2. ______________________________
3. ______________________________

TODAY I FEEL

WRITE OR DRAW ABOUT YOUR FAVORITE PART OF TODAY!

A JOYFUL MOMENT

WHO IS SOMEONE YOU REALLY LIKE SPENDING TIME WITH? WRITE ABOUT SOMETHING FUN YOU TWO HAVE DONE TOGETHER.

DATE: S M T W TH F S ___ ___ ___

I AM THANKFUL FOR

1 ______________________________

2 ______________________________

3 ______________________________

TODAY I FEEL

WRITE OR DRAW ABOUT
YOUR FAVORITE PART OF TODAY!

DATE: S M T W TH F S ____ ____ ____

I AM THANKFUL FOR

1. ____________________
2. ____________________
3. ____________________

TODAY I FEEL

WRITE OR DRAW ABOUT YOUR FAVORITE PART OF TODAY!

DATE: S M T W TH F S ___ ___ ___

I AM THANKFUL FOR

1. ______________________________

2. ______________________________

3. ______________________________

TODAY I FEEL

WRITE OR DRAW ABOUT YOUR FAVORITE PART OF TODAY!

DATE: S M T W TH F S ___ ___ ___

I AM THANKFUL FOR

1 

2 

3

TODAY I FEEL

WRITE OR DRAW ABOUT
YOUR FAVORITE PART OF TODAY!

DATE: S M T W TH F S ___ ___ ___

I AM THANKFUL FOR

1. ______________________

2. ______________________

3. ______________________

TODAY I FEEL

WRITE OR DRAW ABOUT
YOUR FAVORITE PART OF TODAY!

DATE: S M T W TH F S ___ ___ ___

I AM THANKFUL FOR

1 ____________________

2 ____________________

3 ____________________

TODAY I FEEL

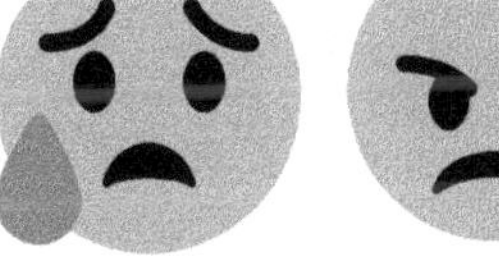

WRITE OR DRAW ABOUT

YOUR FAVORITE PART OF TODAY!

DATE: S M T W TH F S ___ ___ ___

I AM THANKFUL FOR

1 ____________________

2 ____________________

3 ____________________

TODAY I FEEL

WRITE OR DRAW ABOUT YOUR FAVORITE PART OF TODAY!

DATE: S M T W TH F S ___ ___ ___

I AM THANKFUL FOR

1 ______

2 ______

3 ______

TODAY I FEEL

WRITE OR DRAW ABOUT

YOUR FAVORITE PART OF TODAY!

DATE: S M T W TH F S ____ ____ ____

I AM THANKFUL FOR

1. ______________________________

2. ______________________________

3. ______________________________

TODAY I FEEL

WRITE OR DRAW ABOUT
YOUR FAVORITE PART OF TODAY!

A JOYFUL MOMENT

DO YOU KNOW HOW AMAZING YOU ARE? WRITE ABOUT ONE OF YOUR SPECIAL TALENTS AND HOW YOU WOULD LIKE TO SHARE IT WITH OTHERS.

DATE: S M T W TH F S ____ ____ ____

I AM THANKFUL FOR

1. ________________

2. ________________

3. ________________

TODAY I FEEL

WRITE OR DRAW ABOUT YOUR FAVORITE PART OF TODAY!

DATE: S M T W TH F S ___ ___ ___

I AM THANKFUL FOR

1 ______________________

2 ______________________

3 ______________________

TODAY I FEEL

WRITE OR DRAW ABOUT
YOUR FAVORITE PART OF TODAY!

DATE: S M T W TH F S ____ ____ ____

I AM THANKFUL FOR

1. ______________________

2. ______________________

3. ______________________

TODAY I FEEL

WRITE OR DRAW ABOUT YOUR FAVORITE PART OF TODAY!

DATE: S M T W TH F S ___ ___ ___

I AM THANKFUL FOR

1 ______

2 ______

3 ______

TODAY I FEEL

WRITE OR DRAW ABOUT
YOUR FAVORITE PART OF TODAY!

DATE: S M T W TH F S ___ ___ ___

I AM THANKFUL FOR

1 ______________________

2 ______________________

3 ______________________

TODAY I FEEL

WRITE OR DRAW ABOUT
YOUR FAVORITE PART OF TODAY!

DATE: S M T W TH F S ___ ___ ___

I AM THANKFUL FOR

1 ______

2 ______

3 ______

TODAY I FEEL

WRITE OR DRAW ABOUT

YOUR FAVORITE PART OF TODAY!

DATE: S M T W TH F S ___ ___ ___

I AM THANKFUL FOR

1 ___

2 ___

3 ___

TODAY I FEEL

WRITE OR DRAW ABOUT
YOUR FAVORITE PART OF TODAY!

DATE: S M T W TH F S ____ ____ ____

I AM THANKFUL FOR

1. ______________________________

2. ______________________________

3. ______________________________

TODAY I FEEL

WRITE OR DRAW ABOUT

YOUR FAVORITE PART OF TODAY!

DATE: S M T W TH F S ___ ___ ___

I AM THANKFUL FOR

1 ______________________

2 ______________________

3 ______________________

TODAY I FEEL

WRITE OR DRAW ABOUT
YOUR FAVORITE PART OF TODAY!

A JOYFUL MOMENT

WHO IS YOUR FAVORITE TEACHER AND WHY? WRITE THEM A THANK YOU NOTE.

DATE: S M T W TH F S ___ ___ ___

I AM THANKFUL FOR

1. ______________________

2. ______________________

3. ______________________

TODAY I FEEL

WRITE OR DRAW ABOUT

YOUR FAVORITE PART OF TODAY!

DATE: S M T W TH F S ____ ____ ____

I AM THANKFUL FOR

1. ______________________

2. ______________________

3. ______________________

TODAY I FEEL

WRITE OR DRAW ABOUT YOUR FAVORITE PART OF TODAY!

DATE: S M T W TH F S ___ ___ ___

I AM THANKFUL FOR

1 ______

2 ______

3 ______

TODAY I FEEL

WRITE OR DRAW ABOUT
YOUR FAVORITE PART OF TODAY!

DATE: S M T W TH F S ___ ___ ___

I AM THANKFUL FOR

1 ____________________

2 ____________________

3 ____________________

TODAY I FEEL

WRITE OR DRAW ABOUT
YOUR FAVORITE PART OF TODAY!

DATE: S M T W TH F S ____ ____ ____

I AM THANKFUL FOR

1. ________________

2. ________________

3. ________________

TODAY I FEEL

WRITE OR DRAW ABOUT

YOUR FAVORITE PART OF TODAY!

DATE: S M T W TH F S ___ ___ ___

I AM THANKFUL FOR

1. ______________________________
2. ______________________________
3. ______________________________

TODAY I FEEL

WRITE OR DRAW ABOUT YOUR FAVORITE PART OF TODAY!

DATE: S M T W TH F S ___ ___ ___

I AM THANKFUL FOR

3 ______

TODAY I FEEL

WRITE OR DRAW ABOUT
YOUR FAVORITE PART OF TODAY!

DATE: S M T W TH F S ___ ___ ___

I AM THANKFUL FOR

1 ______

2 ______

3 ______

TODAY I FEEL

WRITE OR DRAW ABOUT
YOUR FAVORITE PART OF TODAY!

DATE: S M T W TH F S ___ ___ ___

I AM THANKFUL FOR

1. ______________________________

2. ______________________________

3. ______________________________

TODAY I FEEL

WRITE OR DRAW ABOUT YOUR FAVORITE PART OF TODAY!

A JOYFUL MOMENT

THINK ABOUT A TIME WHEN SOMEONE BROUGHT YOU JOY AND MADE YOU SMILE. HOW CAN YOU MAKE OTHERS SMILE?

DATE: S M T W TH F S ___ ___ ___

I AM THANKFUL FOR

1. ______________________

2. ______________________

3. ______________________

TODAY I FEEL

WRITE OR DRAW ABOUT
YOUR FAVORITE PART OF TODAY!

DATE: S M T W TH F S ____ ____ ____

I AM THANKFUL FOR

1 ______________________________

2 ______________________________

3 ______________________________

TODAY I FEEL

WRITE OR DRAW ABOUT
YOUR FAVORITE PART OF TODAY!

DATE: S M T W TH F S ___ ___ ___

I AM THANKFUL FOR

1 ______________________________

2 ______________________________

3 ______________________________

TODAY I FEEL

WRITE OR DRAW ABOUT
YOUR FAVORITE PART OF TODAY!

DATE: S M T W TH F S ___ ___ ___

I AM THANKFUL FOR

1 ______

2 ______

3 ______

TODAY I FEEL

WRITE OR DRAW ABOUT
YOUR FAVORITE PART OF TODAY!

DATE: S M T W TH F S ____ ____ ____

I AM THANKFUL FOR

1. ____________________

2. ____________________

3. ____________________

TODAY I FEEL

WRITE OR DRAW ABOUT YOUR FAVORITE PART OF TODAY!

DATE: S M T W TH F S ____ ____ ____

I AM THANKFUL FOR

TODAY I FEEL

WRITE OR DRAW ABOUT
YOUR FAVORITE PART OF TODAY!

DATE: S M T W TH F S ____ ____ ____

I AM THANKFUL FOR

1 ______________________________

2 ______________________________

3 ______________________________

TODAY I FEEL

WRITE OR DRAW ABOUT
YOUR FAVORITE PART OF TODAY!

DATE: S M T W TH F S ____ ____ ____

I AM THANKFUL FOR

1 ______________________________

2 ______________________________

3 ______________________________

TODAY I FEEL

WRITE OR DRAW ABOUT YOUR FAVORITE PART OF TODAY!

DATE: S M T W TH F S ___ ___ ___

I AM THANKFUL FOR

1 ______

2 ______

3 ______

TODAY I FEEL

WRITE OR DRAW ABOUT YOUR FAVORITE PART OF TODAY!

A JOYFUL MOMENT

ISN'T IT FUN TO LEARN ABOUT SOMETHING NEW? WRITE ABOUT SOMETHING NEW AND INTERESTING YOU LEARNED THIS WEEK?

DATE: S M T W TH F S ___ ___ ___

I AM THANKFUL FOR

1 ____________________

2 ____________________

3 ____________________

TODAY I FEEL

WRITE OR DRAW ABOUT
YOUR FAVORITE PART OF TODAY!

DATE: S M T W TH F S ____ ____ ____

I AM THANKFUL FOR

1 ______________________________

2 ______________________________

3 ______________________________

TODAY I FEEL

WRITE OR DRAW ABOUT
YOUR FAVORITE PART OF TODAY!

DATE: S M T W TH F S ___ ___ ___

I AM THANKFUL FOR

1 ____________________

2 ____________________

3 ____________________

TODAY I FEEL

WRITE OR DRAW ABOUT
YOUR FAVORITE PART OF TODAY!

DATE: S M T W TH F S ___ ___ ___

I AM THANKFUL FOR

3 ___

TODAY I FEEL

WRITE OR DRAW ABOUT
YOUR FAVORITE PART OF TODAY!

DATE: S M T W TH F S ___ ___ ___

I AM THANKFUL FOR

1 ______________________________

2 ______________________________

3 ______________________________

TODAY I FEEL

WRITE OR DRAW ABOUT
YOUR FAVORITE PART OF TODAY!

DATE: S M T W TH F S ___ ___ ___

I AM THANKFUL FOR

1 ______________________________

2 ______________________________

3 ______________________________

TODAY I FEEL

WRITE OR DRAW ABOUT YOUR FAVORITE PART OF TODAY!

DATE: S M T W TH F S ___ ___ ___

I AM THANKFUL FOR

1 ____________________

2 ____________________

3 ____________________

TODAY I FEEL

WRITE OR DRAW ABOUT
YOUR FAVORITE PART OF TODAY!

DATE: S M T W TH F S ___ ___ ___

I AM THANKFUL FOR

1 ______

2 ______

3 ______

TODAY I FEEL

WRITE OR DRAW ABOUT
YOUR FAVORITE PART OF TODAY!

DATE: S M T W TH F S ____ ____ ____

I AM THANKFUL FOR

1. ______________________________

2. ______________________________

3. ______________________________

TODAY I FEEL

WRITE OR DRAW ABOUT
YOUR FAVORITE PART OF TODAY!

A JOYFUL MOMENT

WHAT IS SOMETHING THAT MAKES YOU FEEL HAPPY EVEN WHEN YOU ARE FEELING DOWN?

DATE: S M T W TH F S ___ ___ ___

I AM THANKFUL FOR

1 ____________________

2 ____________________

3 ____________________

TODAY I FEEL

WRITE OR DRAW ABOUT
YOUR FAVORITE PART OF TODAY!

DATE: S M T W TH F S ___ ___ ___

I AM THANKFUL FOR

1 ______

2 ______

3 ______

TODAY I FEEL

WRITE OR DRAW ABOUT

YOUR FAVORITE PART OF TODAY!

DATE: S M T W TH F S ___ ___ ___

I AM THANKFUL FOR

1 ______________________________

2 ______________________________

3 ______________________________

TODAY I FEEL

WRITE OR DRAW ABOUT
YOUR FAVORITE PART OF TODAY!

DATE: S M T W TH F S ____ ____ ____

I AM THANKFUL FOR

1. ______

2. ______

3. ______

TODAY I FEEL

WRITE OR DRAW ABOUT
YOUR FAVORITE PART OF TODAY!

DATE: S M T W TH F S ___ ___ ___

I AM THANKFUL FOR

1 ______________________________

2 ______________________________

3 ______________________________

TODAY I FEEL

WRITE OR DRAW ABOUT

YOUR FAVORITE PART OF TODAY!

DATE: S M T W TH F S ___ ___ ___

I AM THANKFUL FOR

1. ______________________________

2. ______________________________

3. ______________________________

TODAY I FEEL

WRITE OR DRAW ABOUT YOUR FAVORITE PART OF TODAY!

DATE: S M T W TH F S ____ ____ ____

I AM THANKFUL FOR

1. ________________________________
2. ________________________________
3. ________________________________

TODAY I FEEL

WRITE OR DRAW ABOUT

YOUR FAVORITE PART OF TODAY!

DATE: S M T W TH F S ____ ____ ____

I AM THANKFUL FOR

1. ______________________________

2. ______________________________

3. ______________________________

TODAY I FEEL

WRITE OR DRAW ABOUT YOUR FAVORITE PART OF TODAY!

DATE: S M T W TH F S ___ ___ ___

I AM THANKFUL FOR

1 ____________________

2 ____________________

3 ____________________

TODAY I FEEL

WRITE OR DRAW ABOUT
YOUR FAVORITE PART OF TODAY!

A JOYFUL MOMENT

TAKE A LOOK IN THE MIRROR AND WRITE DOWN WHAT YOU LOVE ABOUT YOURSELF.

DATE: S M T W TH F S ___ ___ ___

I AM THANKFUL FOR

1 ____________________

2 ____________________

3 ____________________

TODAY I FEEL

WRITE OR DRAW ABOUT
YOUR FAVORITE PART OF TODAY!

DATE: S M T W TH F S ____ ____ ____

I AM THANKFUL FOR

1. ________________________________

2. ________________________________

3. ________________________________

TODAY I FEEL

WRITE OR DRAW ABOUT
YOUR FAVORITE PART OF TODAY!

DATE: S M T W TH F S ___ ___ ___

I AM THANKFUL FOR

1 ______________________

2 ______________________

3 ______________________

TODAY I FEEL

WRITE OR DRAW ABOUT
YOUR FAVORITE PART OF TODAY!

DATE: S M T W TH F S ____ ____ ____

I AM THANKFUL FOR

1. ________________________________

2. ________________________________

3. ________________________________

TODAY I FEEL

WRITE OR DRAW ABOUT YOUR FAVORITE PART OF TODAY!

DATE: S M T W TH F S ___ ___ ___

I AM THANKFUL FOR

1 ______________________________

2 ______________________________

3 ______________________________

TODAY I FEEL

WRITE OR DRAW ABOUT
YOUR FAVORITE PART OF TODAY!

DATE: S M T W TH F S ____ ____ ____

I AM THANKFUL FOR

1 ______________________________

2 ______________________________

3 ______________________________

TODAY I FEEL

WRITE OR DRAW ABOUT
YOUR FAVORITE PART OF TODAY!

DATE: S M T W TH F S ___ ___ ___

I AM THANKFUL FOR

1 ________________

2 ________________

3 ________________

TODAY I FEEL

WRITE OR DRAW ABOUT

YOUR FAVORITE PART OF TODAY!

DATE: S M T W TH F S ___ ___ ___

I AM THANKFUL FOR

1. ______________________________

2. ______________________________

3. ______________________________

TODAY I FEEL

WRITE OR DRAW ABOUT
YOUR FAVORITE PART OF TODAY!

DATE: S M T W TH F S ___ ___ ___

I AM THANKFUL FOR

1 ______________________________

2 ______________________________

3 ______________________________

TODAY I FEEL

WRITE OR DRAW ABOUT
YOUR FAVORITE PART OF TODAY!

A JOYFUL MOMENT

WHICH HOLIDAY ARE YOU GRATEFUL FOR?
WHAT IS YOUR FAVORITE THING TO DO
ON THAT DAY?

DATE: S M T W TH F S ___ ___ ___

I AM THANKFUL FOR

1 ____________________

2 ____________________

3 ____________________

TODAY I FEEL

WRITE OR DRAW ABOUT
YOUR FAVORITE PART OF TODAY!

DATE: S M T W TH F S ___ ___ ___

I AM THANKFUL FOR

1 ______________________________

2 ______________________________

3 ______________________________

TODAY I FEEL

WRITE OR DRAW ABOUT
YOUR FAVORITE PART OF TODAY!

DATE: S M T W TH F S ____ ____ ____

I AM THANKFUL FOR

1 ____________________

2 ____________________

3 ____________________

TODAY I FEEL

WRITE OR DRAW ABOUT

YOUR FAVORITE PART OF TODAY!

DATE: S M T W TH F S ___ ___ ___

I AM THANKFUL FOR

1 ______________________________

2 ______________________________

3 ______________________________

TODAY I FEEL

WRITE OR DRAW ABOUT
YOUR FAVORITE PART OF TODAY!

DATE: S M T W TH F S ____ ____ ____

I AM THANKFUL FOR

1 ____________________

2 ____________________

3 ____________________

TODAY I FEEL

WRITE OR DRAW ABOUT
YOUR FAVORITE PART OF TODAY!

DATE: S M T W TH F S ___ ___ ___

I AM THANKFUL FOR

1. ______________________

2. ______________________

3. ______________________

TODAY I FEEL

WRITE OR DRAW ABOUT
YOUR FAVORITE PART OF TODAY!

DATE: S M T W TH F S ___ ___ ___

I AM THANKFUL FOR

1 ______________________

2 ______________________

3 ______________________

TODAY I FEEL

WRITE OR DRAW ABOUT YOUR FAVORITE PART OF TODAY!

DATE: S M T W TH F S ___ ___ ___

I AM THANKFUL FOR

3 ___

TODAY I FEEL

WRITE OR DRAW ABOUT
YOUR FAVORITE PART OF TODAY!

A JOYFUL MOMENT

WHICH ONE OF YOUR FIVE SENSES ARE YOU MOST THANKFUL FOR? WHAT ARE SOME THINGS YOU LOVE TO DO WITH THAT SENSE?

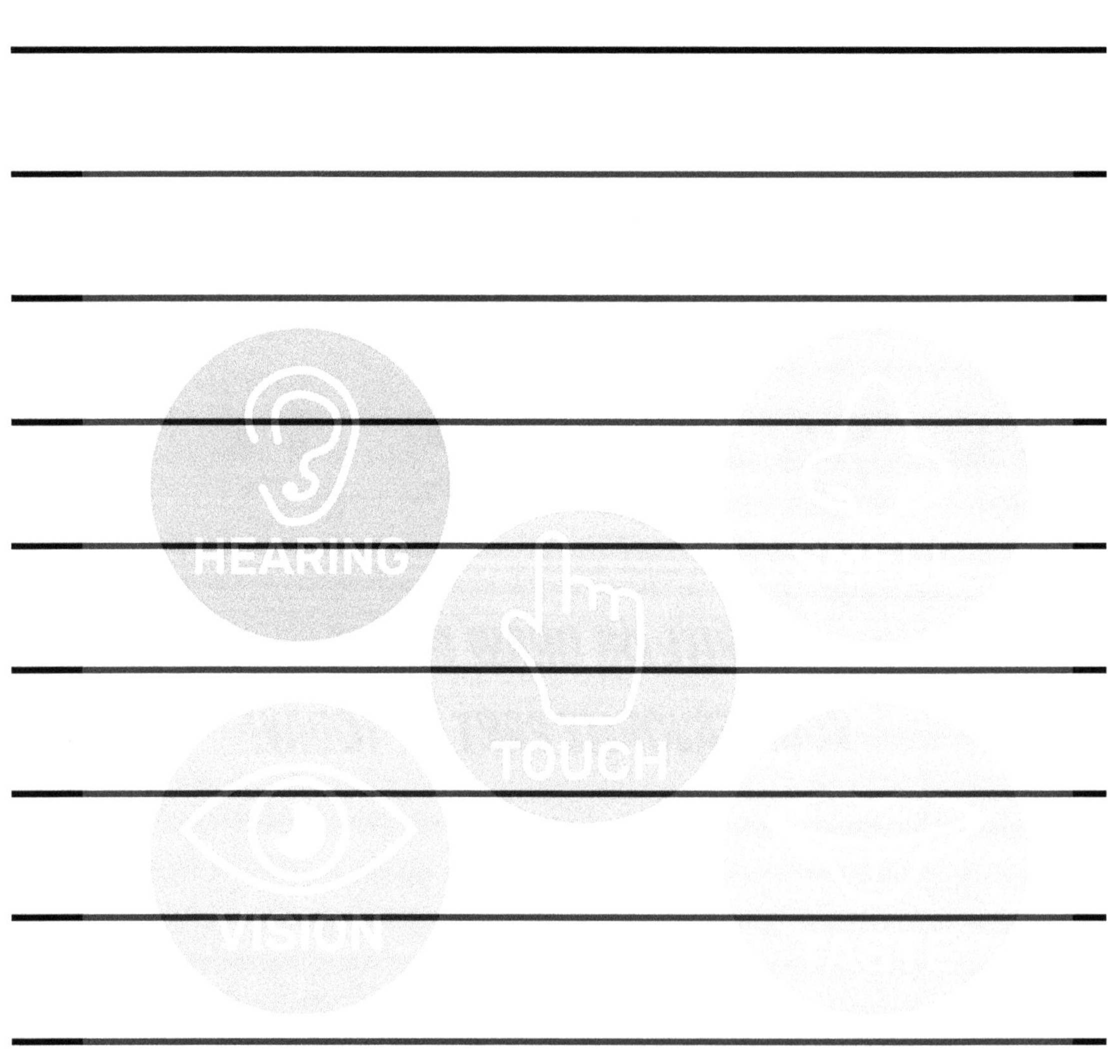

www.ingramcontent.com/pod-product-compliance
Ingram Content Group UK Ltd.
Pitfield, Milton Keynes, MK11 3LW, UK
UKHW051129260726
13967UKWH00010B/2948

9 781955 574051